My Jewish Year

Cath Senker

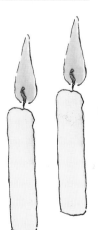

HODDER
Wayland

an imprint of Hodder Children's Books

Titles in this series

My Buddhist Year • My Christian Year • My Hindu Year
My Jewish Year • My Muslim Year • My Sikh Year

Conceived and produced for Hodder Wayland by

Nutshell
MEDIA

Intergen House, 65-67 Western Road, Hove BN3 2JQ, UK
www.nutshellmedialtd.co.uk

Editor: Polly Goodman
Inside designer and illustrator: Peta Morey
Cover designer: Tim Mayer
Consultant: Jonathan Gorsky, The Council of Christians & Jews

Published in Great Britain in 2002 by Hodder Wayland, an imprint of Hodder Children's Books.

This paperback edition published in 2004
© 2002 Hodder Wayland

British Library Cataloguing in Publication Data
Senker, Cath
My Jewish year. - (A year of religious festivals)
1. Fasts and feasts - Judaism - Juvenile literature
I. Title
394.2'67

ISBN 0 7502 4061 X

Printed in China

Hodder Children's Books
A division of Hodder Headline Limited
338 Euston Road, London NW1 3BH

Acknowledgements: The author would like to thank Fiona Sharpe, Winston Pickett, Adam Pickett
and Lexi Pickett for all their help in the preparation of this book.

Picture Acknowledgements:
Art Directors and Trip Photo Library 6 (E. James), 7, 8 (I. Genut), 11 (A. Tovy), 12, 19, 21 (H. Rogers);
Circa Photo Library 14, 16, 18, 24 (Barrie Searle); Eye Ubiquitous 15 (Chris Fairclough), 25 (David
Cohen); Heather Angel 20; Nutshell Media Title page (Andy Johnstone), 5 (Yiorgos Nikiteas), 20 (Andy
Johnstone); World Religions 4 (Christine Osborne); Panos 27 (Nancy Durrell Mckenna); Sonia Halliday
17, 22, 26 (David Silverman); Z. Radovan, Jerusalem Cover, 13.

Cover photograph: Children dressed up for the Purim festival in Israel.
Title page: Dressed up for Purim in France.

Contents

The Jewish people

Jewish people believe there is one God.
He is everywhere and watches over them.

Jews follow the teachings written down
in the Torah, the Jewish holy book.
They also follow many other teachings
of their rabbis.

**A rabbi in synagogue.
Rabbis teach the
Jewish tradition.**

This is Adam. He has written a diary about the Jewish festivals.

Adam's diary

Wednesday 13 August

My name's Adam Pickett. I'm 8 years old. I live with my mum, dad and sister Lexi – she's 5. We have a cat called Poppet. I like playing football. Lexi and I go to the Torah Academy School, which is a Jewish school. I love all the Jewish festivals.

There are rules to help people live a Jewish life. There are also many festivals. Some festivals remind people of events in Jewish history. Others celebrate God's work in creating the world.

The Jewish symbol is the Star of David.

Shabbat in the home

Every Friday

Shabbat is the Jewish day of rest. It is also called the Sabbath. Shabbat lasts from just before sunset on Friday evening until it is dark on Saturday evening.

On Friday evening, families spend time together. Before the sun sets, the mother lights two candles and says a blessing.

Two candles are lit to welcome in Shabbat.

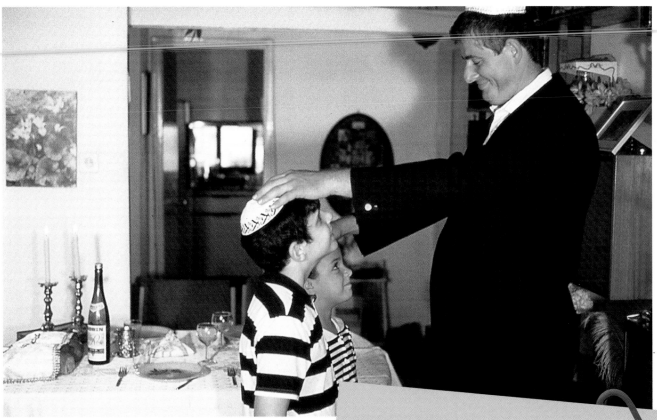

This father is blessing his children. The table is set for the Shabbat meal.

The father blesses his children. He says a blessing called Kiddush over wine.

He blesses the special bread, called challah. Then the family eats a delicious meal.

Adam's diary
Saturday 16 August

Last night Dad came home early from work for Shabbat. This Friday we had visitors, too. Mum lit the candles and Lexi helped her. Lexi has her own small candles to light. Dad made Kiddush over the wine. We had chicken for dinner (sometimes we have lamb chops). We chatted about what we did in the week.

Shabbat in the synagogue

Every Saturday

Jewish people do not work on Shabbat. They spend a quiet day with their family.

On Saturday morning they go to synagogue. The rabbi reads from the Torah and gives a sermon. Everyone wishes each other 'Shabbat shalom' – 'good Sabbath'.

These boys are praying in synagogue. The prayer book is written in Hebrew, the Jewish holy language.

This is the Havdalah ceremony. When the candle is lit, Shabbat is over.

Adam's diary
Sunday 17 August

Yesterday I went to synagogue with my dad. The rabbi read the Parsha, the weekly part of the Torah. In the evening we had the Havdalah ceremony to end Shabbat. We lit a candle and put spices on a plate. The spices showed that the sweetness of Shabbat was ending. Everyone sang songs. I held the candle mostly but Lexi had a turn, too.

After synagogue, families have a meal at home. They spend the afternoon reading the Torah, telling each other stories and relaxing. At the end of Shabbat there is the Havdalah ceremony.

Rosh Hashanah

September

Rosh Hashanah is the Jewish New Year. In synagogue the rabbi blows a ram's horn called a shofar. It is like a 'wake-up call'.

At Rosh Hashanah, Jewish people think about what they have done wrong over the past year.

The rabbi is blowing the shofar in synagogue.

This family is eating a special meal for Rosh Hashanah. There are dates, pumpkin jam and other sweet fruits.

At home, people eat apples with sweet honey, or food made from carrots or pumpkins. The colour orange stands for good luck. Everyone wishes each other a sweet and happy New Year.

Adam's diary
Saturday 27 September

Yesterday, the rabbi at our school blew the shofar in the hall for Rosh Hashanah. Today we ate apples dipped in honey. I don't like apples and I don't really like honey either, but we always eat them at Rosh Hashanah. I went to synagogue with mum, dad and Lexi. We had loads of visitors and we visited other people too. We ate a lot!

Yom Kippur

September or October

Yom Kippur is the holiest day of the Jewish year. People think about any bad things that they have done over the past year. They say sorry and ask God to forgive them.

On Yom Kippur, mothers of Jewish families light candles just before sunset and the holy day begins. The synagogue is packed. Everyone prays to God.

Adults do not eat or drink for 25 hours. This is called fasting. Children may fast for just part of the day.

The Yom Kippur candle is lit at the beginning of the fast. It stays alight until the end.

Some Jewish men wear a white robe called a kittel for Yom Kippur. It is a sign of being pure.

Adam's diary
Monday 6 October

God has three books: the good book, the bad book and the middle book. He weighs up the good and the bad things you've done on his scales. If you've had a good year you go in the good book. If you've had an OK year you go in the middle book. And if you've had a bad year you go in the bad book. But God will always forgive you.

Sukkot

September or October

At Sukkot, Jewish people remember their ancestors by building an outdoor shelter. It is called a sukkah.

During Sukkot, families eat their meals in the sukkah. In hot countries they sleep in them, too. They remember how the Jewish people left Egypt long ago.

This boy holds the four plants that are used at Sukkot prayers.

These children are decorating the roof of their sukkah with fruit.

The Jews travelled through the desert from Egypt to Israel. When they stopped, they built small huts for shelter. They covered the huts with leaves from palm trees.

Adam's diary

Sunday 12 October

Yesterday was the first day of Sukkot. We made a tiny sukkah at home out of wafers, peanut butter and pretzels. I went to see my friend Asher's sukkah. It was really groovy. His family had decorated it with CDs! We had a sukkah at school, which we decorated with kaleidoscope patterns we had drawn ourselves. The teachers hung up fruit too and we shook the Sukkot plants.

Simchat Torah

October

Simchat Torah is a happy day. The Torah is carried around the synagogue. Everyone sings and dances.

The Torah is very precious. Every synagogue has one made from long scrolls.

The end of each scroll is stitched to a wooden pole. The pole is used to wind up the scroll.

At Simchat Torah, people parade the Torah scrolls through the synagogue.

People use a pointer called a yad so they don't touch the precious Torah. The Torah is written in Hebrew.

Adam's diary
Saturday 18 October

Today it was Simchat Torah. We danced around in the synagogue. We sang songs as well. It was really good fun. We all got bags of sweets at the end. At school I studied the Torah. I learnt some more Hebrew words. I can read some Hebrew already and say a few blessings.

A part of the Torah is read every week in synagogue. At Simchat Torah, the rabbi reads the last part of the Torah and then starts again from the beginning.

Hanukkah

December

At Hanukkah, Jews remember the time long ago when their ancestors stood up to their Greek rulers. Their rulers wanted them to worship many gods. They ruined the Jews' beautiful temple in Jerusalem.

These children are learning to light the Hanukkah candles. Then they will eat some fried doughnuts.

The hanukiah has eight branches and an extra one for the lighting candle.

A brave Jewish group called the Maccabees fought the Greeks and won. They cleaned the temple in Jerusalem and lit their holy lamps. They thought there was only enough oil for one day, but it lasted for eight days – a miracle!

At Hanukkah, Jews light candles on a special candle holder called a hanukiah.

Adam's diary
Sunday 28 December

Last week at school we made our own hanukiahs out of clay for Hanukkah. When they were dry we painted them. At home we lit a big hanukiah. We ate latkes (pancakes) fried in oil to remember how in the old days they used oil to light the hanukiah. We got a present every day of Hanukkah, for eight days. It was my birthday at Hanukkah too.

Tu B'Shvat

January or February

This happy festival celebrates nature. It marks the time in Israel when the rainy season is over. Trees start to grow their new fruit.

Some Jewish people plant trees at Tu B'Shvat. They talk about how they can care for the countryside. Many different kinds of fruit are tasted, too.

This fig tree is growing new fruit.

Jewish people believe that God brings the changes in the seasons. He looks after nature all the time.

Jewish people in many countries plant a tree at Tu B'Shvat. These people are planting a cherry tree in England.

Adam's diary
Sunday 8 February

Yesterday it was Tu B'Shvat, which is all about trees. People plant new trees. Two years ago the whole school planted trees and I helped. This year we held a Tu B'Shvat meal with lots of different fruits, like pomegranate. I didn't eat them myself because I don't like any fruit or vegetables, except for broccoli.

Purim

February or March

Purim is the most cheerful day in the Jewish year. It celebrates the Jewish people who lived in Persia over 2,400 years ago.

At that time, the king of Persia had a chief minister called Haman. He hated the Jews and wanted to kill them. The king agreed. But he didn't know his wife, Esther, was Jewish.

Jewish people eat cakes called 'Haman's ears' in memory of the Purim story.

These children in France are wearing fancy dress for Purim.

Esther risked her life by asking the king to save the Jews. Luckily the king changed his mind and the evil Haman was hanged.

Adam's diary
Sunday 7 March

Today it was Purim. I love Purim because we get to dress up. At school on Friday I wore a Greek god costume. My mum made it out of a pillow-case. At school Rabbi Efune read the story of Esther in Hebrew. The story was written in English on the board with pictures. Every time we heard the name 'Haman' we banged the chairs.

Pesach

March or April

Pesach is a happy festival. It is also called Passover. It celebrates the Jews' escape from Egypt long ago.

Over 3,000 years ago, the Jewish people were slaves in Egypt. Their leader, Moses, asked the pharaoh to let the Jews go, but he refused.

A family group at Seder night. They are reading the story of Pesach. Then they will eat a special meal.

The Seder plate. It holds special foods that are used to help tell the story of Pesach.

Adam's diary
Wednesday 7 April

Last night was the start of Pesach. We went to Seder night, bringing our own plagues! We took toy frogs and locusts, and red plastic noses to pretend they were boils. When the Jews left Egypt, they didn't have enough time to make proper bread. The dough went hard and flat, like matzah. That's why we eat matzah every Pesach.

Then the Egyptians were struck by ten terrible plagues. The last one killed their eldest sons.

In the end, the pharaoh told the Jews to leave. There was no time to bake proper bread. So they grabbed flat bread that had not yet risen and quickly left.

Shavuot

May or June

Shavuot is a joyful event. It celebrates the day when God gave the Torah to the Jewish people. This happened seven weeks after they had escaped from Egypt.

At Shavuot, some Jews stay up all night studying the Torah. People decorate the synagogue with flowers. They eat foods made with milk, such as cheesecake and milk pudding.

Here you can see cheesecake (at the front) and cheese-filled pancakes called blintzes (at the back).

Shavuot is also a harvest festival. These people in Israel are celebrating the wheat harvest in the fields.

Young children are given their first Bible storybooks at Shavuot.

Adam's diary
Thursday 27 May

Yesterday was Shavuot. We ate cheesecake and Mum made pancakes filled with cheese. The grown-ups stayed up all night to pray. That's because the night when God gave the Torah to the Jewish people, they arrived late. To make up for it, people study the Torah all night.

Jewish calendar

September (2 days)

Rosh Hashanah

This festival marks the Jewish New Year.

September/October (1 day)

Yom Kippur

People ask God to forgive them for things they have done wrong.

September/October (7 or 8 days)

Sukkot

Families build huts and live in them for a week.

October (1 day)

Simchat Torah

People show their love for the Torah.

December (8 days)

Hanukkah

People light candles to remember how the Jews got their Temple back.

January/February (1 day)

Tu B'Shvat (New Year for Trees)

Jews plant trees and think about how to care for nature.

February/March (1 day)

Purim

People dress up. They hear how Esther helped to save the Jews from the wicked Haman.

March/April (7 or 8 days)

Pesach

People celebrate the Jews' escape from Egypt. They eat matzah instead of bread.

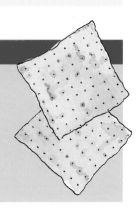

May/June (1 or 2 days)

Shavuot

This festival celebrates God giving the Torah to Moses.

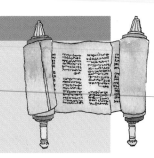

Glossary

blessing A prayer to ask God to protect someone or to thank God for something.

fast To go without food.

hanukiah A candleholder for nine candles. One candle is used to light the others.

Havdalah A ceremony at the end of Shabbat when blessings are said over wine, spices and a candle.

Kiddush A blessing said over a cup of wine at the beginning of Shabbat and festival meals.

kittel A white robe that men wear over their clothes for Yom Kippur. White is a sign of being pure. The men will be pure when they have said sorry for any bad things they have done.

latkes Potato pancakes.

locusts Large insects that fly in big groups and eat all the plants in an area.

matzah A thin cracker made of flour and water.

pharaoh A ruler of Ancient Egypt.

plague An illness that spreads quickly and kills many people. Also, a large number of animals that come into an area and cause damage.

pomegranate A juicy red fruit that contains many seeds.

rabbi A Jewish religious teacher and leader.

scroll A long roll of paper for writing on.

Seder A meal with a religious ceremony. It usually means the Seder at Pesach.

Shabbat Also called the Sabbath. This is the Jewish day of rest, every Saturday.

sermon A talk, usually about a religious topic, given by a religious leader.

shofar A ram's horn that is blown at the time of Rosh Hashanah.

sukkah An outdoor hut with at least three sides and a roof of leaves.

synagogue A building where Jewish people meet, pray and study.

Torah The first five books of the Bible. It can also mean all the Jewish teachings.

Notes for teachers

pp4–5 Jewish people believe that God created the universe and everything that happens in it depends on Him. The word 'Torah' can mean the first five books of the Bible plus Nevi'im (Prophets) and Ketuvim (holy writings). It can also refer to the whole body of teachings that explain the Torah. These teachings include guidance on all aspects of Jewish life, for example, the dietary laws that say Jews should not eat pig meat or consume milk and meat together.

pp6–7 All Jewish festival days start just before sunset and last until dark the following evening. Jews believe that God created the world in six days and the seventh, the Sabbath, was a day of rest. During Shabbat, no work may be done. Lighting the candles marks the beginning of Shabbat. The father recites Kiddush over the wine, a blessing thanking God for Shabbat. The bread is blessed too; Jews always thank God before they eat. The Shabbat meal is relaxed and pleasurable.

pp8–9 The synagogue is the heart of the community, where people go to pray, study and participate in communal activities. A rabbi is a teacher; one of his or her most important roles is to run study classes. In synagogue the rabbi leads prayers, reads from the Torah and gives sermons on issues related to Judaism. Havdalah means 'separation'; the ceremony separates Shabbat from the rest of the week. Blessings are said over wine, spices and a candle.

pp10–11 Rosh Hashanah is the beginning of the season of repentance. At this festival, people remember how God created the world and look forward to the coming year. The blowing of the shofar tells them that it is time to examine their consciences. It also recalls Abraham's willingness to sacrifice his son, Isaac, for God and reminds them that they too should obey God. At the celebratory meal, a blessing for a sweet New Year is recited over slices of apple dipped in honey.

pp12–13 People fast to keep their minds on God and spiritual matters. It is a penance for misdeeds and helps them to identify with starving and suffering people. Judaism accepts that people make mistakes; they should be able to confess to them, show repentance and pray for forgiveness. Yom Kippur is actually a happy occasion because people welcome the chance to repent their wrongdoing. The explanation of God weighing up people's deeds comes from the Midrash, a collection of explanatory texts that explain how to apply the Torah to everyday life.

pp14–15 The sukkah must have at least three sides and a roof of leaves thick enough to provide shade. Recreating the living conditions of their ancestors helps Jews to feel part of an ancient people. At Sukkot, four plants – palm, myrtle, willow and etrog (rather like a lemon) – are used each day during prayer (except on Shabbat). They are waved in all four directions and upwards and downwards, to symbolize God's presence everywhere. Sukkot is also a harvest festival.

pp16–17 Simchat Torah means 'Rejoicing of the Law'. Every week in synagogue, a portion of the Torah is read. At Simchat Torah, the last verses of Deuteronomy are read, completing the reading of the Torah, and the rabbi starts again with the first chapter of Genesis. Usually only one or two Torah scrolls are taken out of the Ark for reading; on this festival all the scrolls are removed. The Torah may be paraded outdoors as well as around the synagogue. There is great merriment.

pp18–19 Hanukkah commemorates the victory in the 2nd century BCE of the Maccabean Revolt, a Jewish uprising against their Syrian-Greek rulers, who wanted them to stop practising Judaism and adopt the Greek way of life. In 165 BCE the Temple was rededicated by lighting an oil lamp. There was enough oil for only one day, but miraculously the oil lasted for eight days, by which time new supplies of oil had been prepared. In memory of the miracle, Jews light a nine-branched candlestick called a hanukiah. On the first night one candle is lit using an extra 'servant' candle. On the second night another candle is lit until on the eighth and final night, all eight are alight.

pp20–21 The origins of Tu B'Shvat lie in the Torah, which commanded farmers to set aside a tithe for priests and the poor. The festival marked the cut-off date for tithes of fruit. At this time of year, trees in Israel were beginning to grow new fruit. Fruit harvested after Tu B'Shvat would be tithed in the following year. Jews eat fruit from Israel to celebrate Tu B'Shvat. The festival has now become a focus for discussing the protection of the environment.

pp22–3 Purim means 'lots'. Haman cast lots (like throwing a dice), to decide on which day to slaughter the Jews. He wanted them to be murdered without being able to defend themselves. Persuaded by Esther, the king still allowed the Jews' enemies to attack them but permitted them to fight back. They were victorious. At Purim, the Book of Esther is read aloud. Children, wearing fancy dress, hiss and boo when Haman's name is mentioned. People exchange food presents (this is called mishloach manot) and give donations to charity.

pp24–5 Before Pesach, Jewish homes are thoroughly cleaned to remove all leavened products (grain products that rise during baking). They must not eat these foods during Pesach. On Seder night, the whole family gathers to read the Hagadah, the book that tells the Pesach story. A ceremonial plate holds symbolic foods referring to parts of the story. A piece of matzah called the afikomen (dessert) is hidden; it represents the last hurried meal before the Jews left Egypt. The finder receives a reward. The afikomen is eaten after dinner.

pp26–7 There is no special ritual associated with Shavuot; the giving of the Torah on Mount Sinai was so important that no action could adequately represent it. Some Jews study the Torah all night, as Adam explains. Tradition says that dairy foods are eaten because when the Jews first received the laws concerning meat preparation, they didn't quite understand them. They ate other foods until they did. Shavuot is also a harvest festival; in Israel the wheat crop is gathered at this time.

p28 The Jewish year is based on lunar months, so there are just over twelve in a calendar year. To keep the festivals in their season, some years have an extra 'leap' month. Orthodox Jews outside Israel have two-day festivals, while Reform, Progressive and Israeli Jews celebrate one day.

Other resources

Artefacts

Articles of Faith, Resource House, Kay Street, Bury BL9 6BU. Tel. 0161 763 6232.
Jewish Education Bureau, 8 Westcombe Avenue, Leeds LS8 2BS. Tel 01132 663613/ 0870 7300532.
Religion in Evidence, 28b Nunnbrook Road Industrial Estate, Huthwaite, Notts NG17 2HU. Tel. 0800 318686.

Books to read

Celebrate: Passover by Mike Hirst (Hodder Wayland, 2002)
Celebration Stories: The Taste of Winter by Adéle Geras (Hodder Wayland, 2002)
Celebration Stories: Waiting for Elijah by Ann Jungman (Hodder Wayland, 2002)
Holy Places: the Western Wall and other Jewish Holy Places by Mandy Ross (Heinemann Library, 2003)
Jewish Festival Tales by Saviour Pirotta (Hodder Wayland, 2001)
Jewish Festivals Cookbook by Ronnie Randall (Hodder Wayland, 2001)
Jewish Synagogue by Laurie Rosenberg (A & C Black, 2000)
Places of Worship: Synagogues by Sharman Kadish (Heinemann, 1999)
My Belief: Jew by C. Lawton (Franklin Watts, 2001)

Photopacks

Jews photopack, by the Westhill Project, available from Adrian Leech, Westhill RE Centre, Birmingham Tel. 0121 415 2258. E-mail: a.leech@bham.ac.uk
Living Religions: Judaism posterpack and booklet (Nelson Thornes)

Websites

www.holidays.net/highholydays/ – information about Rosh Hashanah and Yom Kippur.
www.jewfaq.org/ - general information about Judaism at different levels from basic to advanced.
www.theresite.org.uk Includes curriculum resources and IT in RE pages with details of CD-Roms, software and videos, and TV and radio programmes.
www.underfives.co.uk/events.html Lists the dates of main festivals for all major religions.

Index